Does This Thought Serve Me?

Serve Me?

The key to a happier life!

Written by Catherine A. Haala

Illustrator: Jacqueline Rodriguez
with Blueberry Illustrations

Editor: Bradley Jones

Does This Thought Serve Me? The key to a happier life!

Haala Publishing
Sleepy Eye, MN

ISBN: 978-1-956726-00-8

Dedicated to my brothers and sisters ...

Gerald Haala
Christine Deibele
Cherie Haala
Cory Haala
and
their families!

I love you and I always will!

Does This Thought Serve Me?

The key to a happier life!

Written by Catherine A. Haala

Thoughts, thoughts, thoughts …

I have so many thoughts each and every day …

How do I decide which thoughts should go
and which thoughts should stay?

It's really quite simple you know …

I keep the thoughts that I want more of and ...

I let the others go!

I am worthy ...

I am free …
I control my thoughts, they don't control me!

I look that thought
right in the eye ...

I look it up ...

I look it down ...

8

I look that thought
inside out ...

I look that thought
all around!

9

Does this thought serve me ...
Yes or no?

If it doesn't, I let it go!

"Wheeeee**eee!**
I release you with love …
I set you free …
Thoughts that don't serve me
have no power over me!"

If that thought returns or wants to stay ...
I stand strong, I relax, I get clear ...
It's only a thought, I have nothing to fear!

I *choose* to forgive …
I let go of anger, resentment and blame …
I simply don't want to attract more of the same!

I release limitations **BIG** and small …
I release them now, I release them ALL!

"You are not who I am ...
You are not who I **choose** to be!"

"Limitations"

"Wheeeeeee!"
"I release you with love ...
I set you free ...
Thoughts that don't serve me have no
power over me!"

"I am POWERFUL!"

"I am Freeeeeee!
I *choose only* thoughts that serve me!"

"I accept perfect guidance from
PERFECT LOVE!"

"What is it that serves me?
What do I want more of?"

**I *choose* new thought seeds that serve me …
I plant them deep down inside …**

I easily, effortlessly and joyfully
tend to them with pride!

I THINK
I BELIEVE
I KNOW

That in perfect time, those seeds
GROW, GROW, GROW!

Now new thoughts that
serve me are here to stay ...

Thoughts that seed more and
more positivity into my life and
into the universe each and every day!

Peaceful, loving, grateful …

Thought-filled ME!

www.ingramcontent.com/pod-product-compliance
Lightning Source LLC
Chambersburg PA
CBHW042146240326
41723CB00013B/606